BEAUMARIS CASTLE

Arnold Taylor CBE, DLitt, FBA

Contents

Series Editor David M. Robinson *BSc, PhD, FSA*
Designed by Icon Design

First Published by Her Majesty's Stationery Office (Cardiff) 1980
Second Edition Published by Cadw (Cardiff) 1985; Revised 1988
Fourth Edition 1999

© *Cadw: Welsh Historic Monuments (Crown Copyright),*
Crown Building, Cathays Park, Cardiff, CF1 3NQ.

Printed in Great Britain by South Western Printers

ISBN 1 85760 101 7

'BEAU MAREYS'
THE CASTLE ON THE
FAIR MARSH

The castle on the 'fair marsh', *Beau Mareys* in Norman-French, was begun on 18 April 1295. It was the last of the great royal castles with which — from 1277 onwards — King Edward I (1272–1307) of England ringed the north Wales seaboard, from Flint to Aberystwyth. Like the other strongholds at Rhuddlan, Aberystwyth and Harlech, it was designed on the concentric plan, with the main courtyard of the castle surrounded by a narrow enclosing ward and both of them in turn protected by a wide outer moat.

And yet the site chosen for Beaumaris — on level marshy ground, not very far from the water's edge — enabled its likely architect, Master James of St George (d. 1308), to invest its concentric layout with a degree of symmetry not attained at any of its predecessors. It also allowed him to fill the encircling moat with a controlled supply of tidal water. It is this combination of near-perfect symmetrical planning and water defences that gives Beaumaris its most striking and remarkable characteristics.

This said, in another respect the castle is sometimes thought a little disappointing. Lacking the surmounting turrets of Harlech, or Conwy, or Caernarfon, the skyline at Beaumaris is visually rather less impressive. The Anglesey stronghold has a certain squatness, and it somehow fails to dominate its surroundings. This is because, although the work of building went on more or less continuously for some thirty-five years, when it finally ceased in the 1330s the great towers of the inner ward were still without their top storeys, while the turrets — which seem to have been intended to rise here in even greater profusion than at the earlier castles — were never so much as begun.

There was great initial progress with the works in 1295 and 1296, and a contemporary estimate of the labour requirement for the latter year refers to the employment of no fewer than 200 quarrymen, 400 stonemasons and 2,000 minor workmen. The same record enables us to say with some precision what parts of the castle were built first. In fact, with the help of this documentary evidence, together with that provided by an important account of 1306, we are able to trace the successive stages of work throughout almost the entire structure.

Figures preserved in the annual accounts of the exchequer at Westminster (the Pipe Rolls) and in the north Wales chamberlains' account (compiled year by year at Caernarfon) show a total cost for the building of Beaumaris Castle of about £14,500 between 1295 and 1330. Over £6,000 of this was spent in the first six months, rising to over £11,000 in the first five years.

The castle has relatively little later history to record. Any sieges it may have had to withstand, for example, were not of the kind which add so much to the story of Harlech. Like all the north Wales castles it was held for the king in the Civil War; with its surrender to Parliament in June 1646 its active life was at an end. Some partial works of demolition are known to have been carried out thereafter, but most of the structure that was built in the years before and after 1300 has remained standing until our own time.

Situated on the 'fair marsh', near the south-eastern tip of the Isle of Anglesey, and with the mountains of Snowdonia as its verdant backdrop, Beaumaris was the last of the great royal castles raised by King Edward I (1272–1307) in north Wales.

A HISTORY OF THE CASTLE

INTRODUCTION

In March 1284, when the death of Llywelyn ap Gruffudd (d. 1282) near Builth and execution of his brother, Dafydd (d. 1283), at Shrewsbury had lately brought to an end the rule of the native Welsh princes, King Edward I laid down in the Statute of Rhuddlan the pattern of a new English-type administration based on shires and counties. These were to embrace and supersede the historic *cantrefi* and *commotes* of Gwynedd. Two of the new shires, Caernarvon and Merioneth, had as their administrative centres the castles of Caernarfon and Harlech, both (like Conwy) newly begun in the spring and summer of 1283. The third shire, Anglesey, at first had no new castle; but from the

THE CASTLES OF KING EDWARD I IN WALES 1277–95

Castles built or wholly rebuilt by King Edward I

Welsh castles repaired by King Edward I

Lordship castles built or rebuilt for King Edward I

Castles of the first war of Welsh independence, 1276–77

Castles of the second war of Welsh independence, 1282–83

beginnings its sheriff, Roger de Pulesdon, was given charge of the manor of Llanfaes. And it was to be within the boundaries of Llanfaes that the new castle of Beaumaris was eventually to begin to rise in 1295.

Very probably the decision to build it was taken, and its site chosen, during a week the king spent at Llanfaes in August 1283, at the very time when Conwy, Harlech and Caernarfon were all just begun. A decision not to proceed immediately with the actual work may well have been taken at the same time; the enormous demands made by the simultaneous construction of the three mainland castles (and in the case of Conwy and Caernarfon of the town walls also), as well as by other works like the repair of Aberystwyth, Criccieth and Castell y Bere, must have stretched the English labour and financial resources to the utmost. The projected castle on the island of Anglesey could take a lower priority.

The position thus selected for the future castle lay close beside the existing Welsh town of Llanfaes, already long the principal trading port of the island. Since 1237 it had been endowed with a priory of Franciscan friars, in whose church lay King John (1199–1216) of England's daughter, Joan (d. 1237), wife of Llywelyn the Great (d. 1240). Equidistant by water between the castles of Conwy and Caernarfon, Llanfaes also lay on the old overland route from Chester to Holyhead by way of Rhuddlan, Aberconwy and Llangefni. It was the place to which travellers to Ireland were ferried at low tide across the channel of the Menai Strait after riding out over the Lavan sands from Aber. No other place in Anglesey was so well suited to become the centre of its English administration and trade, as well as filling at the same time a notable gap in the chain of coastal castles that extended from Flint to Aberystwyth.

By the end of the 1280s, Conwy and Harlech were finished and Caernarfon well advanced. In terms of building resources, the way therefore now lay open to undertake the building of the final castle in the series planned in 1283, and the founding of the new town annexed to it. Then, in the autumn of

Right: King Edward I of England probably determined upon building a castle on Anglesey as early as 1283. The decision to proceed with Beaumaris followed a furious and widespread Welsh revolt over the winter of 1294–95. In this late thirteenth-century manuscript illustration, the autocratic and short-tempered Edward is shown seated facing his archbishops and a group of clergy (British Library, Cotton Vitellius Ms. A XIII, f. 6v).

1294, following a decade of simmering resentment, the Welsh — led in the north by Madog ap Llywelyn — rose in a furious and widespread revolt. The people of Arfon sacked and severely damaged Caernarfon itself, with many casualties inflicted on the English. The sheriff of Anglesey, none other than the king's favourite, Roger de Pulesdon, was hanged. The revolt at first took Edward by surprise, but his response was speedy and overwhelmingly thorough.

Resistance was quelled in a critical campaign in the winter of 1294–95, the reassertion of English power being immediately demonstrated by the eviction of the entire Welsh population of Llanfaes

and the commencement on the 'fair marsh' nearby of the king's new castle and town of Beaumaris (Norman-French '*Beau Mareys*', Latin '*de Bello Marisco*'). The Welsh inhabitants were moved to a newly established settlement, situated some twelve miles (19.3km) away near the south-west tip of the island, and to which the name of Newborough was given.

Long before the building of Beaumaris, Llanfaes had been Anglesey's principal trading port. In 1237, it was endowed with a priory of Franciscans, in whose church lay Joan (d. 1237), wife of Llywelyn the Great (d. 1240). Princess Joan's coffin was moved to Beaumaris parish church after the priory's dissolution in the late 1530s.

Begun in 1283, Caernarfon was the jewel in the crown of Edward I's castles in north Wales, and was built to echo the Emperor Constantine's Roman city of Constantinople.

Jutting out on its rugged promontory towards Tremadog bay, with the mountains of Snowdonia in the distance, Harlech is perhaps the most familiar of Edward I's Welsh strongholds.

Raised almost in their entirety between 1283 and 1287, the castle and town walls at Conwy were intended as much as a centre from which to administer the new order of Edward I in north Wales as a symbol of awesome military domination.

One of a number of native Welsh castles appropriated by Edward I, Criccieth became an important link in the king's chain of north Wales fortifications (Skyscan Balloon Photography, for Cadw: Welsh Historic Monuments).

[facsimile of medieval building accounts manuscript — handwritten Latin text]

THE BUILDING OF THE CASTLE: 1295–98

The most astonishing thing about the building of Beaumaris is the speed with which the work got into its stride in the summer of 1295. Its direction was in the hands of Master James of St George, the master of the king's works in Wales. Like the king himself, he was probably by then a man in his middle fifties, and already had to his credit the building of the castles of Builth and Aberystwyth, Rhuddlan and Flint, Conwy and Harlech, and — to the point at which it then stood — of Caernarfon. Such was the practical experience that Master James had at his command, ready to bring to bear with maximum effect the moment the tide of victory over revolt should enable the English to reoccupy Anglesey's south-eastern coast.

The reoccupation took place on or about 10 April, from which date until 6 May the king made his headquarters at Llanfaes. There, on 17 April, Master James received 'by his own hands' an advance of 60s. for necessaries 'for the new castle'. On the following day, the newly appointed clerk of works, Walter of Winchester, received the first of a series of payments which, in the course of the next six months, were to reach a figure of over £7,800, some £6,736 of it for the works of '*the new castle of Beau Mareys*'. All through the summer and autumn the money poured in from Chester and Rhuddlan, from Conwy and Ireland, and from the exchequer at Westminster.

Income was matched by outlay. In the twenty-four weeks from 18 April to 29 September 1295 the bills passed the £6,000 mark. In this short summer season the carriage of materials alone cost over £2,100, more than the total recorded expenditure on this item at Conwy, Harlech or Caernarfon throughout the 1280s. Here at Beaumaris, most of the building stone had to be fetched from a distance by water, both from Penmon and from beyond Benllech, and a naval force was kept in being till mid-July 'to keep the sea between Snowdon and Anglesey'. In the same period the wages of workmen digging trenches and excavating the moat, and also — at the king's order — putting up a barricade around the site of the new castle, amounted to no less than £1,468 12s. 0d., indicating that their numbers throughout the summer must have averaged something like 1,800 men. Similarly

Above: *A section of the 1295 building accounts for Beaumaris Castle. Amongst items mentioned, are wages for diggers and minor workmen digging trenches and excavating the moat (Public Record Office, E 372/158).*

Left: *As master of the king's works in Wales, James of St George (d. 1308), was to oversee enormous expenditure at Beaumaris. In the first six months alone, the bills exceeded £6,000. In this mid-thirteenth-century manuscript illustration, a king is seen directing his master mason (British Library, Cotton Nero Ms. D I, f. 23v).*

A LETTER OF 1296

This letter from James of St George and Walter of Winchester was sent from Conwy to the treasurer and barons of the exchequer at Westminister.

Aberconewey,
27 February 1296

To their very dear lordships the treasurer and barons of the exchequer of our lord the king, James of St George and Walter of Winchester send greeting and due reverence.

Sirs,
As our lord the king has commanded us, by letters of the exchequer, to let you have a clear picture of all aspects of the state of works at Beaumaris, so that you may be able to lay down the level of work

(ordiner lestat de loevre) for this coming season as may seem best to your, we write to inform you that the work we are doing is very costly and we need a great deal of money.

You should know:

(i)   That we have kept on masons, stone cutters, quarrymen and minor workmen all through the winter, and are still employing them, for making mortar and breaking up stone for lime; we have had carts bringing this stone to the site and bringing timber for erecting the buildings in which we are

all now living inside the castle; we also have 1,000 carpenters, smiths, plasterers and navvies, quite apart from a mounted garrison of 10 men accounting for 70s. a week, 20 cross-bowmen who add another 47s. 10d., and 100 infantry who take a further £6 2s. 6d.

(ii)   That when this letter was written we were short of £500, for both workmen and garrison. The men's pay has been and still is very much in arrear, and we are having the greatest difficulty in keeping them because they simply have nothing to live on.

stonemasons' wages totalling £1,005, and quarriers' totalling £636, point to numbers in these categories of 450 and 375 men respectively. The tonnage of stone quarried and shipped, and worked and laid by them, must have been immense. The quantities of materials other than stone are itemized in the surviving accounts and some details may be given here: 2,428 tons of sea-coal, for burning lime; 640 quarters of charcoal; 42 masons' axes; 3,277 boards; ropes, cords and chains; 8 loads of lead; 160 pounds of tin; 314 'bends' of iron; and 105,000 assorted nails.

There must already have been much to see when the king came back in July to inspect the results of the work over the first two and a half months. This time Edward stayed not at Llanfaes, but at Beaumaris itself. Here, on two summer evenings, in a setting of temporary thatch-roofed buildings erected 'within the castle', with the great walls and towers laid out and beginning to rise around them, the records give us a glimpse across the centuries of the king taking his ease after the day's work and listening to the playing of a harpist named Adam of Clitheroe.

Left: *The tonnage of stone quarried, shipped, carved and laid by the Beaumaris workforce must have been immense. In the short summer season of 1295, there may have been up to 450 stonemasons and 375 quarriers employed on the project. In this near-contemporary manuscript illustration, a mason is shown laying mortar with a trowel, while another is seen cutting stone with a hammer and chisel, and another produces angles with the aid of a set square (Pierpont Morgan Library, New York, Ms. 638, f. 3).*

By great good fortune, there has survived a letter sent in February 1296 by James of St George and Walter of Winchester to the officials of the exchequer at Westminster. Their letter reported in detail what had been achieved since the previous April, and gave an estimate of how much money would be needed if the pace of construction was to be maintained through the new building season that would shortly be commencing.

It seems that the curtain wall of the inner ward already stood in places to a height of twenty-eight feet (8.5m), and was nowhere less than twenty feet (6.1m). Four of the main inner ward towers had been begun, namely two on either side of the north and south gatehouse passages, and four gates were in position and were shut and locked at night; each gate-passage was to have three portcullises. In addition, work on ten smaller towers out of the sixteen which would eventually flank the curtain of the outer ward had been started. The letter also implies that work was in hand on the castle dock, which would allow a 40-ton vessel to come fully laden right up to the gate of the castle at high tide.

All this progress required the efforts of 400 masons, 200 quarrymen, 30 smiths, an unspecified number of carpenters, and 2,000 labourers. Some 30 boats, 60 waggons and 100 carts had been employed in bringing stone to the site and transporting coal for the lime-kilns. And to keep a similar labour force employed through the coming year it would require the expenditure of at least £250

(iii)   That if our lord the king wants the work to be finished as quickly as it should be on the scale on which it has commenced, we could not make do with less than £250 a week throughout the season; with it, this season could see the work well advanced. If, however, you feel we cannot have so much money, let us know, and we will put the workmen at your disposal according to whatever you think will be the best profit of our lord the king.

As for the progress of the work, we have sent a previous report to the king. We can tell you that some of it already stands about 28 feet high and even where it is lowest it is 20 feet. We have begun 10 of the outer and four of the inner towers, that is the two for each of the two gatehouse passages. Four gates have been hung and are shut and locked every night, and each gateway is to have three portcullises. You should also know that at high tide a 40-ton vessel will be able to come fully laden right up to the castle gateway; so much have we been able to do in spite of all the Welshmen.

In case you should wonder where so much money could go in a week, we would have you know that we have needed — and shall continue to need — 400 masons, both cutters and layers, together with 2,000 minor workmen, 100 carts, 60 wagons and 30 boats bringing stone and sea-coal; 200 quarrymen; 30 smiths; and carpenters for putting in the joists and floor-boards and other necessary jobs. All this takes no account of the garrison mentioned above, nor of purchases of materials, of which there will have to be a great quantity.

As to how things are in the land of Wales, we still cannot be any too sure.

But, as you well know, Welshmen are Welshmen, and you need to understand them properly; if, which God forbid, there is a war with France and Scotland, we shall need to watch them all the more closely.

You may be assured, dear sirs, that we shall make it our business to give satisfaction in everything.

May God protect your dearest lordships.

PS — And, Sirs, for God's sake be quick with the money for the works, as much as ever our lord the king wills; otherwise everything done up till now will have been of no avail.

(Public Record Office, E 101/5/18, no. 11)

a week (other figures show that in the first summer it had in fact been running at about £270 a week). Master James and Walter of Winchester told the exchequer officials that money was needed urgently. Payments were already £500 in arrear, and men were apparently leaving the site because they had nothing to live on.

In the event, the 1295 level of expenditure was not approached again. In the second summer, from May to September 1296, it reached only some £2,132, less than one third of the previous year's figure. Money continued to run short, and on 7 May there was not enough to pay all the workmen. There were also debts for materials, which continued to be required in enormous quantities, as for example 16,200 freestones quarried by four contractors, and 32,583 tons of stone transported by sea to the castle. But the king's increasing commitments to Scotland

It is very difficult to be sure of the background and training of the many master masons involved in Edward I's castle and town works at Beaumaris during the late thirteenth and fourteenth centuries. It seems likely, however, that apart from James of St George and Nicholas de Derneford, other masters who had worked on so-called 'court style' projects were also involved. In the nave windows of the parish church of St Mary and St Nicholas, for example, the tracery — with its spikes and split cusps — is of Kentish motif form. It betrays a mason drafted in for the royal works in north Wales.

inevitably diminished the resources available for Wales, and expenditure dwindled until after the end of the 1298 building season it appears to have almost ceased. We have only the record of a single assignment of £100 for the works in October 1300.

THE BUILDING OF THE CASTLE 1306–30

No more is heard of Beaumaris until 1306. In that year a newly appointed constable, John of Metfield, reported on the state of the far from finished castle and made recommendations for improving its security. The indications are that, up to this time, the outer curtain and its towers had not advanced beyond the work done in the summer of 1295; in other words only ten towers (numbered 1 to 10 on the plan at the end of the guide), with the corresponding lengths of curtain wall, had even been begun, and still stood only to a height of about eight feet (2.4m) above the water of the moat. Meanwhile, towers 11 to 16, with their linking lengths of curtain wall, had yet to be started. In short, on the north and north-west sides, the castle was still left without any outer ring of defence.

In all, Metfield enumerated seven 'grievous defaults'. His report (in Norman-French), stated that a good, strong barbican was needed to cover the gate towards the dock, and at the other gate either the same thing or a good barricade (*a la porte deuer Le Porth ... une bone Barbecane e forte, e al autre ensemest o bones barres*). In addition, the portcullises (those mentioned in the letter of 1296) were still needed. And it would still be necessary to complete the closing in of the castle on the north and north-west sides, either with a wall of stone or, failing that, a strong palisade. Metfield's other recommendations were to repair the gates and change their locks; to scour and deepen the moat; to clean out the drains and the basements of the towers (rather suggesting that they may have been then, as now, open to the sky); and to repair and roof over the latrines, evidently then, as now, likewise exposed to the elements.

What, then, was done? To begin with, the barbican was duly built against the front of the south gatehouse, intentionally impeding direct access to the gate-passage. The round rear arch in the barbican is a Savoyard feature, suggesting completion before 1309, the year in which Master James of St George died. At much the same time, the entrance to the north gatehouse, still the more exposed of the two, was blocked up: in May 1306 a

Top: *Although the building work at Beaumaris went on more or less continuously for some thirty-five years, from 1295 until the 1330s, when it finally ceased, the castle still remained very much incomplete. The great towers of the inner ward were left without their upper storeys, and their turrets were never so much as begun. Moreover, the massive north gatehouse was left without much of its second floor, and the back of the south gatehouse barely rose above foundation level. This imaginative reconstruction gives an impression of the completed castle as it was originally conceived by King Edward's master masons (Illustration by Terry Ball, 1987).*

Left: *A detail from a late medieval manuscript illumination showing a mason at work with a combing-chisel (Bibliothéque Nationale, Paris, Ms. Latin 4915, f. 46v).*

mason and four labourers were paid 'for obstructing the gate towards the field' (*obstruenti portam versus campum*), and remains of the blocking walls they built against the sides of the gate-passage can still be seen today. These works — the barbican in front of the south gate and the barricade in the north gate-passage — would have compensated for the absence of the six portcullises, most of which could not have been installed until later, when the superstructures needed for hanging and working them had been built to the requisite height.

The urgent improvement of the unfinished defences at this time was part of a programme for bringing the castle into full commission in a period when there was fear of the Scots making common cause with the Welsh and effecting a landing on the north Wales coast. In April 1306, the constable went on a forty-day visit to London to buy armour and other supplies for the castle garrison, his purchases including a breviary for use in the chapel and twenty-two baldrics, or belts covered with red leather. In June, a mason named William de Kyrkebi was paid 3*s.* 9*d.* for shaping 180 round stones at the Penmon quarry 'for the prince's engines in the castle'; in August he received 3*s.* 4*d.* for another 160 round stones 'for the trebuchets in the castle'.

James of St George was succeeded at Beaumaris by Master Nicholas de Derneford, who had come to join Master James after previously working at St Augustine's Abbey, Bristol, the abbey of Burton in Staffordshire and Repton Priory in Derbyshire. It is perhaps to Derneford's hand that we should ascribe the unusual form of the window heads on the courtyard face of the north gatehouse (pp. 29–30). From 1323 his responsibilities at Beaumaris were embraced within those of the wider office of master of the king's works in north Wales, which he continued to exercise until 1331, by which date it is to be inferred that the Beaumaris works — at least as a continuous operation — were finally halted.

In general, the work of the previous twenty years must have been a gradual building-up, first at one point and then at another, from where things had been left in 1298. Attention was focussed on both the inner and outer rings of walls and towers, and on the inward part of the north gatehouse. One major new undertaking was evidently the closing of the gap on the north and north-west section of the outer circuit of walls, including the Llanfaes Gate and towers 13 to 16. There are references to completing ten-and-a-half perches of the moat between 1312 and 1315, and in 1317 to a payment for twelve perches of moat. These may well relate to the stretches of the moat alongside the new sections of wall and towers. Even then, the front of the Llanfaes Gate was left unfinished towards the field, and possibly it is this gate which is referred to in a stray document which as late as 1402 speaks of some old lead tanks being melted down to provide roofing for 'the new tower in the outer ward'. Probably another new undertaking of 1310–30 was the construction of the spur wall on the east side of the dock known as the Gunners Walk.

Over the castle as a whole, the curtain walls — both outer and inner — were completed to the full height of their corbelled parapets. So, too, apart from those of the north gate, were the outer towers. But for the most part the great towers of the inner ward only reached a little above the floor level of their top storeys, at which point they were left unfinished. The turrets, which would have surmounted them and given the castle as picturesque a skyline as Conwy, Harlech and Caernarfon castles, were not even begun.

RECORDED WORKS EXPENDITURE AT BEAUMARIS CASTLE 1295–1330

THE LATER MIDDLE AGES

Proof that, structurally speaking, the incomplete castle we see today is still very much the building at the stage at which it was left in 1330, and is not the result of decay, depredation or demolition in later periods, is provided by a report which has come down to us of a survey of Beaumaris and other castles made by William de Emeldon on behalf of Edward, the Black Prince (d. 1376), in 1343. Emeldon estimated that to bring Beaumaris to anywhere near completion would need the expenditure of at least £684, a very considerable sum. Nearly half of this would be needed to build the south gatehouse, still scarcely begun towards the courtyard; finishing the north gatehouse would cost £100, and the Chapel Tower £128; the other towers could simply have their roofs repaired at the existing level at a cost of £5 to £10 each. The survey says nothing of a need to erect the buildings in the courtyard whose fireplaces are still to be seen in the east and west curtains; it may well be, therefore,

The walls and still uncompleted towers of Beaumaris were put to their first serious test more than a century after they were first began. In the closing months of 1403, the castle was besieged by the Welsh rebel forces of Owain Glyn Dŵr. This late fifteenth-century manuscript illustration depicts a siege on moated castle walls (British Library, Royal Ms. 14, E IV, f. 252).

that these had in fact already been built before 1330, and that their disappearance belongs to a later phase of the castle's history.

During the rest of the fourteenth and most of the fifteenth centuries, the north Wales chamberlains' accounts periodically record minor sums spent on maintenance, but there is no firm evidence of work of any consequence being carried out. Nevertheless, in the years of tension leading to the Glyn Dŵr revolt of the early fifteenth century, defence of the

In this survey of 1343, William de Emeldon estimated that £684 was required to bring Beaumaris anywhere near completion (Public Record Office, E 163/4/42).

castle was by no means taken for granted. In 1389, for example, twenty men were placed in Beaumaris on the chamberlain's order, 'because of enemies at sea'. During the height of the revolt itself, in the closing months of 1403, the castle was certainly besieged by the Welsh. There is a record, too, which suggests a mill was built within the castle, presumably increasing the garrison's capacity to withstand an extended siege. In any case, in June 1405 a relief raid was launched from Ireland, putting the Welsh rebels in Anglesey to flight and leading to the recapture of the castle.

Thereafter, in the long term, the amount of maintenance done was not sufficient to arrest the gradual process of continuing deterioration, especially of the leadwork and roof timbers

throughout the castle. By 1534 'there was scarcely a single chamber in Beaumaris Castle where a man could lie dry', and four years later all four north Wales castles were reported to be '*much ruynous and ferre in decay for lacke of tymely reparacons*'.

Writing from Beaumaris to the king's secretary, Thomas Cromwell (d. 1540), on 9 April 1539, Sir Richard Bulkeley (d. 1546/47) reported that:

The royal castles of north Wales are unfurnished and have neither guns nor powder, nor other artillery, apart from eight or ten small pieces in Bewmares possessed by the writer. Has provided three barrels of gunpowder, some shot, forty bows and forthy sheaves of arrows, with as many coats of fence and sallets and splinters, at his own cost; this is inadequate for such a fortress. Conwey,

---

WILLIAM DE EMELDON'S SURVEY OF 1343

In June 1343, William de Emeldon was appointed to investigate the state of the king's principal castles in Wales, five castles in the north, and nine in the south. The report of the enquiry on the state of the fabric of Beaumaris being as follows:

By inquisition held there in the presence of the said William on 3 August 1343, into the defects of the said castle of Beaumaris, it is found:

1. *That a certain chamber over the Gate next the Sea is dilapidated and ruinous and can be repaired and mended for £7, viz. for stonework £2, for timber and carpentry £3, and for leadwork and other necessaries £2.*

2. *That the roofs and floors of two chambers in the double tower ('le Gemell Tour') are badly dilapidated and ruinous through rotted timbers and lack of roofing, and can be repaired and mended for £35, viz. £25 for masonry and stonework, £8 for woodwork, and £2 for leadwork and other necessaries.*

3. *That the roof of the hall and of the chamber of the same hall can be repaired and mended in lead for 13s. 4d.*

William de Emeldon's survey of Beaumaris Castle was conducted on behalf of Edward, the Black Prince (d. 1376) in August 1343. In this fourteenth-century manuscript illustration, Edward is shown being invested with the duchy of Aquitaine by his father, King Edward III (British Library, Cotton Nero Ms. D VI, f.31).

4. *That a tower called 'Rustycoker' is ruinous for want of a roof and can be roofed and mended for an estimated £8, viz. £4 for stonework and £4 for leadwork and other necessaries.*

5. *That a tower called 'le Chapeltoure' which is begun and not finished can be completed for £128, all works included.*

6. *That a tower called 'Pilardesbath' is dilapidated and ruinous owing to the rotting of its timber and roof, and can be roofed with slates (cum tegulis) and mended where other wise necessary for £10, viz. £5 for stonework, £3 for carpentry and £2 for slates and other works.*

7. *That a tower called 'le Gyntour' is in very great need of repair, and can be repaired and mended for £10, viz £5 for stonework, £3 for timber and carpentry, and £2 for leadwork and other necessaries.*

8. *That Three (sic) towers called 'Gemelles Toures' (literally 'twin' or 'double' towers) above the inner gatehouse (super portam interiorem) of the said castle can be roofed and mended for £15, viz. £9 for carpentry and woodwork and £6 for lead for the roofs.*

9. *That a tower called 'le Mideltoure' can be roofed and repaired for £5, viz. £3 for timber and carpentry and £2 for roofing in lead.*

Carn' and Hardlach castles have nothing in them to defend them for one hour. If enemies secure them 'hit wold cost his majestie a hundreth thowsand of his pounds and the losse of mayny a man affor' they shuld be gotten agayn'. Anglesey is but a night's sailing from Scotland ... beseeches a couple of gunners and some good ordnance and powder to defend the King's house in Bewmares'.

The Bulkeley family settled in Anglesey during the late Middle Ages and was to play a significant role in the fortunes of Beaumaris Castle through to the twentieth century. A sixteenth-century brass in the parish church of St Mary and St Nicholas commemorates Richard and Elizabeth Bulkeley. Richard is described in the inscription as 'a prudent merchant of this little town'.

---

10. *That a tower which stands at the corner of the castle towards the meadow (in angulo castri versus pratum) can be repaired and mended for £10, viz. £5 for stonework, £3 for timber and carpentry, and £2 for lead for the roof.*

11. *That 30 perches (rode) of the walls of the said castle which are partly ruinous can be repaired for £30.*

12. *That it is estimated that two towers and two chambers on the inner gatehouse of the said castle, which are begun and not finished cannot be completed for less than £200 for stone and stonework, £80 for timber and carpentry, and £40 for leadwork and other necessaries.*

13. *That the kitchen, which is dilapidated and ruinous for lack of repair and want of a roof, cannot be repaired and mended for less than 10 marks (£6 13s. 4d.) for all works.*

14. *To complete two towers above the hall to height of (blank in manuscript) including the height of the existing towers as they now stand (cum turribus assistentibus), £100 for stone and stonework.*

> *Sum of the defects of the wall, houses, towers and other buildings of the said castle, £684 6s. 8d.*

(Public Record Office, E 163/4/42)

THE SURVEY INTERPRETED

Some of the foregoing paragraphs are more easily identifiable than others. The first paragraph is self explanatory, while paragraph eleven also seems more likely to refer to the outer than to the inner curtain wall. Paragraphs four and six, placed as they are in sequence on either side of the Chapel Tower, are likely to relate to the towers on either side of it, that is the north-east and south-east towers, but which of these was called 'Rustycoker' and which 'Pilardesbathe' is impossible to say, nor can the names themselves be satisfactorily explained. The placing of paragraph seven before, and of paragraph ten immediately after the middle tower paragraph similarly suggests that the 'tower at the corner towards the meadow' must be the north-west tower, and by elimination 'le Gyntour' would thus seem to be the south-west tower; the name may be Welsh 'gwyn' tower, that is white tower. It is to be noted that of all these six towers only one, the Chapel Tower, is recommended for completion, at an estimated cost of £128. It was evidently considered that the others need only be made good as they stand, at costs estimated at from £5 to £10 each.

Besides the estimate for the Chapel Tower, there are three other estimates for work involving resumed construction in stone. The largest of these is in paragraph twelve, and this with its very high figure of £320 must surely represent the cost of completing the building of the south gatehouse. Paragraph fourteen, at £100

for stonework only, must correspondingly relate to the north gatehouse, and more particularly to the carrying of its two half-built staircase towers up to their full planned height. Paragraph two seems also likely to refer to the north gatehouse, more particularly to finishing off (and closing off at their backs) the twin towers flanking the outer end of the gate-passage. The hall and chamber named in paragraph three could be either the hall and chamber on the first floor of the rearward part of the north gatehouse, or the hall and chamber whose fireplaces remain in the curtain wall between the north-east tower and the Chapel Tower, but it is not possible to say which of the two is intended. Paragraph eight seems most likely, by the process of elimination, to refer to the built part of the south gatehouse, that is to reroofing at existing level the rooms in its flanking towers with the connecting rooms over the gate-passage between them. The kitchen named in parargraph thirteen is evidently a separate building; it probably stood against the northern part of the west curtain wall.

It seems fairly certain that none of the major items involving the resumption of structural work on buildings previously left unfinished was put in hand. The arched thickening of the outer curtain between the south-west corner and the Gate next the Sea may possibly have resulted from the recommendation made in paragraph eleven. No evidence has survived to show whether any or all of the less expensive repairs to roofs and other areas were affected as a result of the survey or not.

Though less famous than many of its celebrated north Wales neighbours, by the eighteenth century Beaumaris Castle had been transformed into an ivy-clad ruin, beloved by tourists, writers and painters in search of the Romantic. This landscape engraving of the 1740s shows the town and castle in their 'picturesque' setting (Bodleian Library, Oxford, Gough Maps 36, fig. 49).

THE CIVIL WAR AND AFTER

By 1609, when at least parts of Harlech and Caernarfon were still usable, Beaumaris — like Conwy — was officially classified as '*utterlie decayed*'. To remedy this state of affairs Thomas, viscount Bulkeley (d. 1659), was later claimed by his son to have spent £3,000 in repairing the castle in aid of King Charles I (d. 1649) early in the Civil War, action paralleled at Conwy by Archbishop John Williams (d. 1650). From 1643 onwards, both castles occupied key positions in the transit of men and materials from Ireland to the king. For Beaumaris the eventual victory of Parliament culminated in the surrender of the castle by Colonel Richard Bulkeley (d. 1650) to Major-General Thomas Mytton (d. 1656) on 14 June 1646, 'Beaumaris being a place that hath been of very great use to the King'. A short-lived revolt in 1648 only led in Anglesey to a second surrender of Beaumaris to Mytton on 2 October, and a fine of £7,000 levied on the island for its contumacy.

Under the Protectorate, the constableship of the castle was conferred on Major-General John Jones (d. 1660), a near relative by marriage of Oliver Cromwell, who appointed an old Ironside officer

Major-General Thomas Mytton (1597–1656), from England's Worthies … by John Vicars (London 1647). In May 1645, Mytton became the Parliamentary commander in north Wales. Beaumaris was surrendered to the major-general by the 'vain and reckless' Colonel Richard Bulkeley (d. 1650) in June 1646 (British Library)

named Captain Wray as his deputy, and annual expenditure on the garrison in the 1650s is recorded as amounting to £1,703. And in 1657 we have a reference to two of its number being imprisoned '*for stealing ye leads of ye castle*', which suggests a state of dilapidation, if not active partial demolition, at that time. Only a few years later, in 1665, when Lord Conway's agent was supervising the dismantling of Conwy Castle, he wrote from Conwy to his employer in Warwickshire of the dangers and difficulties encountered in taking down the lead roofs there: '*I feare I can have noe workman here that knoweth how to doe it, but I here there is one at Blewmarris that hath taken downe one or two Castels alreadye, and tomorrow I doe intend to send to gett him*'. Taken together, these references point to a similar dismantling in progress at Beaumaris at about the time of the Restoration in 1660.

THE NORTH VIEW OF BEAUMARIS CASTLE, IN THE ISLE OF ANGLESEY.

THIS Castle is situated in a Low and moorish Ground adjoyning to the Sea, opposit to Aberconway. This Place derives its Name Beau-Marish and in Latin Bellomariscus from its fine Situation

A print of Beaumaris Castle in 1742 by Samuel and Nathaniel Buck. The Llanfaes Gate appears in the foreground, and it seems that the castle had survived — apparently unchanged — very much as it had been left in the 1330s (National Library of Wales).

Above: *When, in 1807, the castle ruins were acquired by Thomas James Warren, seventh Lord Bulkeley (d. 1822), they came to be used as an extension of the aristocratic country home. The inner ward, with its ivy-covered walls, seemed particularly appropriate for outings and events like that shown in this 1852 engraving of the north gatehouse by Alfred Sumners (National Library of Wales).*

Left: *As the setting for the 1832 'Royal Eisteddfod', Beaumaris Castle briefly became a symbol of traditional Welsh culture and history. The event was graced by the presence of Her Royal Highness, Victoria, duchess of Kent (d. 1861), mother of the future Queen Victoria. This painting of the duchess by Sir George Hayter (1792–1871) was completed in 1835 (Her Majesty the Queen).*

This may well have been the period, therefore, which saw the removal of the medieval courtyard buildings, as well as the uproofing of the hall in the north gatehouse, and what may have remained of the tower roofs generally. But in terms of detail we are entirely without information both as to how extensive the stone robbing may have been, and as to how late it may have continued. One cannot look at Beaumaris Gaol (built 1829), for example, without some suspicion as to whether all of its building stone was newly quarried for the purpose, or may not in part at least have come from the castle.

At Beaumaris, as elsewhere, the eighteenth century was a time when the castle ruins acquired their ivy mantle and kept the noiseless tenor of their way. Few besides the travellers to Ireland, who continued to pass by the castle until the opening of Thomas Telford's Conwy and Menai bridges in 1826, can have had occasion to observe it. Beaumaris lacked the fame and the Romantic appeal that increasingly attracted artists and writers to the more scenically beautiful castles on the mainland shore. Once, momentarily, in August 1832, the castle came into its own, when the inner ward was the setting for a 'Royal Eisteddfod', graced by the presence of Her Royal Highness, Victoria of Saxe-Coburg, the duchess of Kent (d. 1861), with her thirteen-year-old daughter and future queen, the Princess Victoria.

Meanwhile, as we have observed, the Bulkeleys had been associated with Beaumaris for many years. As Royalist supporters, the family had defended the castle for the king in the 1640s. In fact, a constable of the castle of the name of Bulkeley first appears as early as 1440, and Bulkeleys or Williams-Bulkeleys have held the office almost without a break since the time of the Civil War. And it was in 1807 that the sixth Lord Bulkeley (d. 1822) acquired the ownership of the castle ruins from the Crown for the sum of £735.

By 1925, when Sir Richard Williams-Bulkeley (1862–1942) placed the castle in the guardianship of the Commissioners of Works for preservation as an ancient monument, the moat had long been entirely filled in and the walls were so shrouded in ivy that most of their masonry was scarcely visible. Their clearance and consolidation, and the re-establishment of the moat on the west and part of the north and south sides, were undertaken during the following ten years, and maintenance has continued ever since. In 1987, Beaumaris Castle was inscribed on the World Heritage List as an historic site of outstanding universal value. Today, the site is maintained on behalf of the State by Cadw: Welsh Historic Monuments.

In 1925, Beaumaris Castle was placed in the guardianship of the Commissioners of Works for preservation as an ancient monument. By the following year, when this picture was taken, work on clearance and consolidation was in hand.

A TOUR OF
THE CASTLE

THE CASTLE PLAN

Many castles are lifted up on rocky cliffs or promontories, even though these may sometimes be only a few feet above the sea, as at Caernarfon. Beaumaris on the other hand lies literally at sea level. And, lacking its own distinctive skyline, it is thus denied the distant views that lend enchantment to, say, Rhuddlan and Harlech, or Conwy and Caernarfon. Indeed, it is only with difficulty that the castle can be seen from just across the estuary of the Menai, and the Romantic artists of the late eighteenth century, Paul Sandby and Peter de Wint, J. M. W. Turner and Richard Wilson, all largely passed it by. Nowadays, the great scale and immense strength of its buildings excite the wonder of a host of visitors, and the purpose of the description that follows is to explain why those buildings are planned as they are, and to point out their more interesting features.

First we shall make our way right into the heart of the castle, into the huge inner ward. In doing so, we shall note the various barriers — no fewer than fourteen of them — that would have had to have been encountered by anyone attempting to do the same thing when the castle was in its heyday. We shall then look at the inner ward itself, at the two great gatehouses through which access was gained to it, and at the curtains and corner towers which enclose it. Lastly we shall describe the ring of defences making up the outer ward, with a final look at these outer defences from the outside.

A castle was generally designed as a fortified residence, capable on occasion of accommodating its lord and his suite, in this case the king or the prince. Meanwhile it would be garrisoned under the command of a constable, who was the lord's deputy or lieutenant. At Beaumaris, all the residential accommodation was either in, or in towers attached to, the inner ward. The lines of defence, four in number, were ranged concentrically around it. Taking them in order from the centre they are:

1 The massive curtain walls, thirty-six feet (11m) high and fifteen and a half feet (4.7m) thick;

2 The outer ward, an encircling area of open ground averaging about sixty feet (18.3m) in width and commanded from the battlements of the inner curtain wall;

3 The lower and less massive outer curtain wall, with its eight battlemented sides flanked by twelve battlemented turrets and pierced by two twin-towered gateways;

4 The water-filled moat, now only partially complete, but originally wholly surrounding everything comprised in the inner three lines.

Something of the massive scale of the concentric — walls within walls — structure of the castle may be gleaned from this view at the south-west corner of the outer ward. Although the turrets on the outer line of defence were virtually completed, the great towers of the inner ward were never to rise much above the height to which they survive today.

A BIRD'S-EYE VIEW OF BEAUMARIS CASTLE
FROM THE SOUTH–WEST

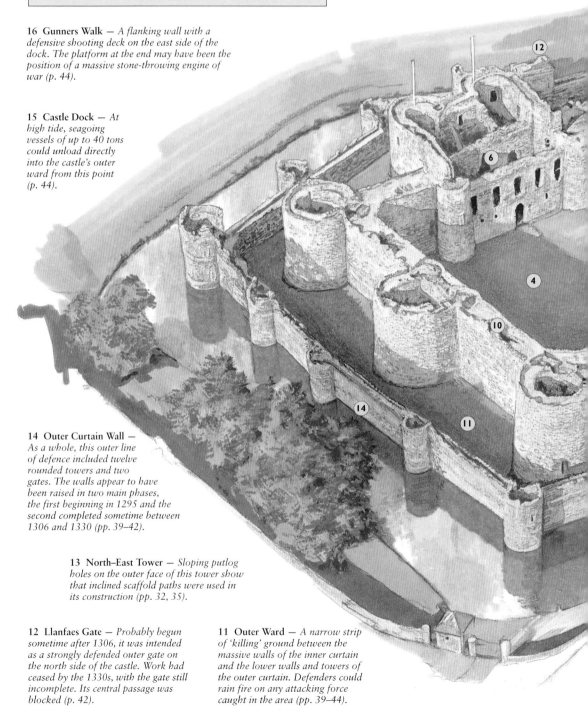

17 Town Wall — *Although planned from the outset, the town walls at Beaumaris were not built until the early fifteenth century. Only the footings, seen at this point, belong to the Edwardian building programme (pp. 40–1).*

16 Gunners Walk — *A flanking wall with a defensive shooting deck on the east side of the dock. The platform at the end may have been the position of a massive stone-throwing engine of war (p. 44).*

15 Castle Dock — *At high tide, seagoing vessels of up to 40 tons could unload directly into the castle's outer ward from this point (p. 44).*

14 Outer Curtain Wall — *As a whole, this outer line of defence included twelve rounded towers and two gates. The walls appear to have been raised in two main phases, the first beginning in 1295 and the second completed sometime between 1306 and 1330 (pp. 39–42).*

13 North–East Tower — *Sloping putlog holes on the outer face of this tower show that inclined scaffold paths were used in its construction (pp. 32, 35).*

12 Llanfaes Gate — *Probably begun sometime after 1306, it was intended as a strongly defended outer gate on the north side of the castle. Work had ceased by the 1330s, with the gate still incomplete. Its central passage was blocked (p. 42).*

11 Outer Ward — *A narrow strip of 'killing' ground between the massive walls of the inner curtain and the lower walls and towers of the outer curtain. Defenders could rain fire on any attacking force caught in the area (pp. 39–44).*

1 Gate Next the Sea — This was the outer entrance to the castle from the medieval town, and is the point where visitors first arrive today. It was defended by a drawbridge, double doors, and 'murder holes' overhead (p. 24).

2 Barbican — Added to the front of the south gatehouse after 1306, it included further obstacles defending the townward entrance to the castle (p. 24).

3 South Gatehouse — As designed, the gate-passage included as many as nine defensive barriers. It was intended to mirror the northern gatehouse, though its rear sections were probably never completed much above foundation level (pp. 24, 31).

4 Inner Ward — The present spaciousness of the great inner ward is somewhat misleading since long ranges of buildings were planned to run along the western and eastern curtain walls (pp. 26–37).

5 Royal Apartments — The backs of two large fireplaces, and access arrangements to the chapel tower suggest that the castle's principal (royal) apartments were situated along the east curtain wall (pp. 26–7).

6 North Gatehouse — Though it stands as but a fragment of the building it was intended to be, this was undoubtedly an imposing structure. To the back, there was a large hall lit by the courtyard windows, and all of the upper rooms in the projecting northern towers provided domestic accommodation (pp. 29–31).

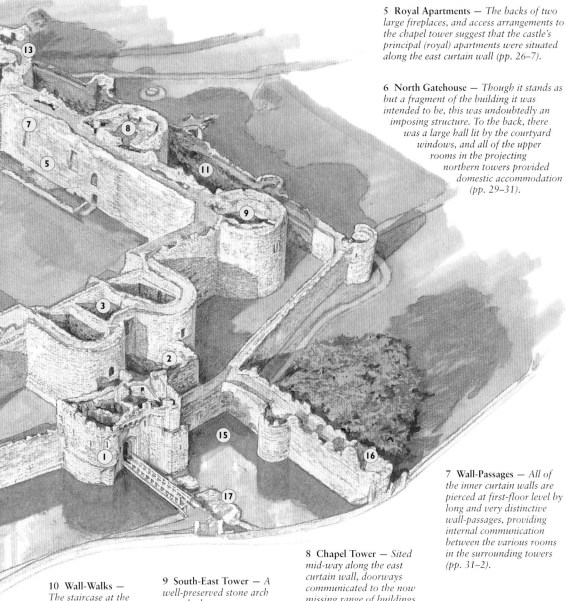

7 Wall-Passages — All of the inner curtain walls are pierced at first-floor level by long and very distinctive wall-passages, providing internal communication between the various rooms in the surrounding towers (pp. 31–2).

8 Chapel Tower — Sited mid-way along the east curtain wall, doorways communicated to the now missing range of buildings within the inner ward. The castle chapel is situated on the first floor (pp. 32–4).

9 South-East Tower — A well-preserved stone arch over the basement may indicate a strong and heavy floor above. The middle, south-west and north-east towers had similar arches. In each case, the principal room was on the first floor (pp. 32, 35).

10 Wall-Walks — The staircase at the south-west corner of the courtyard gives access to the top of the western curtain wall. Latrines were arranged in pairs on all four sides of the ward (pp. 35–7).

(Illustration by John Banbury)

THE GATE NEXT THE SEA, BARBICAN AND SOUTH GATE-PASSAGE

From the ticket office, the path along the south side of the castle leads to a modern timber bridge across the moat. On the other side, the Gate next the Sea contained the first three of those fourteen obstacles which a medieval intruder would have needed to negotiate to gain access to the castle at this point.

To begin with there was a drawbridge, its chains formerly passing through two holes still visible high up within the outer arch. Next there were two parallel 'murder slots' over the gate-passage, and then a heavy two-leaved door of which the drawbar

hole and the stumps of the hinges can still be seen. Passing through the gate, ahead and at right angles are the next two hazards, namely the doorway into the barbican and the barbican itself, its interior commanded by a shooting platform running around the three sides of its wall-head.

The remaining nine barriers were built into the main gatehouse passage. In turn there were: outwards-opening doors, with double drawbar holes on the inside; the first of three portcullises, marked by grooves in the side walls; five parallel 'murder slots' overhead; 'spy

holes' or arrowloops looking through from the guardrooms on either side of the passage; a second portcullis again marked by grooves in the walls; and inwards-opening doors, also with double drawbar holes visible on the inside. Another row of 'murder slots' was situated in the now-missing roof of the next part of the passage, from which doors on either side led to guardrooms, and to the newel stairs in the far corners leading to the upper parts of the gatehouse. Finally, by analogy with the corresponding features of the north gatehouse, came the third portcullis, with yet another 'murder slot' in the arch above it. When all these checks had been safely negotiated, then, and only then, was entrance to be had into the inner ward.

Above: *The castle is approached across a modern wooden bridge leading to the Gate next the Sea. Boats moored in the castle dock could unload their cargo directly into the outer ward through the doorway in the curtain wall to the right of this view.*

Left: *A cutaway reconstruction looking north-east through the barbican and south gatehouse. The western half of the building has been reduced to ground level, and the details of the gate-passage are shown as if they had been completed to the original plan. A medieval attacker would have needed to negotiate up to eleven defensive obstacles to gain entry to the inner ward at this point (Illustration by Chris Jones-Jenkins, 1985; revised 1999).*

Right: *The south gatehouse passage looking out towards the barbican, with the second portcullis groove in the foreground.*

In this aerial view of the castle from the south-east, the wide expanse of the inner ward is particularly striking.

THE INNER WARD

INTERNAL FEATURES

The striking thing about the interior of the inner ward is its size — three-quarters of an acre (0.3ha). It is not difficult to picture it filled, as we are told it was filled in the winter of 1295–96, with huts to house the work force of upwards of 2,000 men engaged in the manifold tasks of construction. Its present spaciousness, however, was originally curtailed, or designed to be curtailed, by long ranges of buildings running the full length of its western and about half the length of its eastern sides, and by a building in the south-east corner. The lower door openings to be seen in the north-east,
south-east and south-west corners, and in the centre of the west side, were all shaped for 'interior doors'. In other words, they were designed to provide access to and from buildings that no longer exist against the east and west curtains. You should note the careful rebating of some of these openings to house flush-fitting doors.

Looking closely at the western side of the ward, you will see a number of other pieces of evidence for these surrounding buildings. At the north end, there is a ground-floor fireplace, and just to the south of it are two small bondings again at ground level. Nearby, in the angle with the north gatehouse, there is a short length of foundation almost six feet (1.8m) wide for the inner
wall of the range. There is also an offset, or narrow ledge, to carry a floor along the whole length of the western curtain. Very probably, the northern part of this lost range contained the kitchen, with the stables to the south. At Conwy they were similarly placed end to end on the opposite side of the courtyard to the hall.

On the east side of the ward, the evidence is provided by a similar (but lower) offset which can be found running along the northern half of the curtain wall [1]. The range as a whole presumably terminated on the line of a return wall near the Chapel Tower, the bonding of which can be seen extending to the full height of the curtain [2]. At the level of the offset are two fine fireplaces [3 and 4], evidently intended to serve rooms of major importance. The windows of these rooms would have been in the now vanished wall towards the courtyard.

Clearly the imposing arched doorway [5] which faces the courtyard at first-floor level would also have been approached from inside the eastern range of buildings. It gave access to a vestibule, which in turn led to the chapel royal. The position of the chapel as an annexe to the range suggests that the latter, including the adjacent north-east tower [6], was intended to provide the castle's principal residential suite. The arrangements would have corresponded as a whole to the royal apartments in the inner ward at Conwy.

Beneath these east range apartments was a low basement [7], and there survives from this a partly blocked opening for light and air towards the north, originally heavily barred where it emerges towards the outer ward. Nearby, the remains of an oven fill the adjacent corner against the north gatehouse.

The existence of a former building in the south-east corner of the inner ward is vouched for by the wall-plaster still adhering to the southern curtain wall. The end wall of this building must have been formed by the east wall of the gatehouse, considerably more of which must therefore have stood at one time than remains today. This fact alone gives rise to doubt as to whether, as has sometimes been suggested, the vanished courtyard buildings were indeed ever built, or whether their absence may not rather reflect the activity of the *'one at blewmaris that hath taken downe one or two Castles alredye'*, as reported by Lord Conway's agent in 1665 (p. 17).

Two other features visible from within the inner ward may be pointed out. The first is a series of three inclined lines of putlog holes sloping up from ground to wall-top level over the whole length of the west curtain. These are best seen from the middle or far side of the courtyard. The holes held the bearer poles of inclined scaffold paths used instead of vertical ladders and cranes for hoisting material at the time of the original building. The careful observer will also notice them in other parts of the castle.

The second feature is the presence at wall-top level of pairs of rounded projections, near to the centre of each of the longer curtains, where they are corbelled out above the main wall face below. They apparently mark the bases of uncompleted turrets, one of which on each side would have contained the stairs to the roof of the adjacent unfinished tower. The position of the castle well, presumably somewhere within the courtyard, has yet to be discovered.

A series of inclined putlog holes along the west curtain of the inner ward indicate the bearer poles of inclined scaffold paths used at the time of the original building. This manuscript illustration, near contemporary with the building at Beaumaris, shows a king watching masons at work alongside an inclined scaffold (British Library, Cotton Nero Ms. E II, f. 73).

A general view showing the northern half of the eastern curtain wall within the inner ward. The numbers highlight those features described in the text.

THE NORTH GATEHOUSE

Imposing though it is, the great north gatehouse at Beaumaris is but a fragment of the building it was intended to be. The overall concept was very similar to that of the near-complete surviving gatehouse designed by Master James twelve years earlier at Harlech, though it was to be a structure of considerably larger dimensions. At Harlech there are six windows on the courtyard side, three to each floor; here at Beaumaris there were to be ten, of which only the lower five were ever built. The upper five, as may still be seen, were never raised beyond the level of their window seats.

In looking at this same courtyard façade, we must also remember that the two corner turrets were initially designed to rise up to double the height to which they stand today. Indeed, if completed, they would have been appreciably taller than the highest surviving parts of the gatehouse. The two rounded towers flanking the outer side of the gatehouse passage are the only towers in the whole inner ward which approach something like their full intended height of about sixty feet (18.3m). They lack only their battlements and their rear walls.

At ground level, running centrally through the gatehouse from north to south, is the heavily defended entrance passage. Its arrangements were very similar to those planned in the south gatehouse. In this case, what appear to be the remains of the blocking structure inserted in 1306 (p. 10) can be seen towards the outer end. On each side of the passage there were intercommunicating rooms for porters and janitors, those to the south giving access to the two turret staircases.

To allow for access from within the castle, when all the doors and portcullises of the passage were closed, there was also an outside stair. As at Harlech, this led up from the courtyard to the rooms on the first floor. In fact, you will see that it communicated through the lower part of the westernmost of the five windows, which accordingly has a lower sill than the others. The former presence of the stair no doubt accounts for the small size of the window openings of the adjoining basement, in contrast to the single large opening which exists on the other side of the gate-passage.

Above: *The first-floor windows in the north gatehouse were originally mullioned and transomed. The transom survives in the easternmost opening. There is a perceptible difference in the jamb mouldings between the upper and lower parts of the windows.*

Left: *Although the inner façade of the great north gatehouse is imposing as it stands, it is but a fragment of the designer's original concept. There was to have been a second floor, with a further row of five handsome windows, and the whole was to be surmounted by a battlement stage with the two round flanking towers rising even higher.*

All five first-floor windows were originally mullioned and transomed, as may be seen from the surviving transom in the easternmost window. Notice, however, that there is a perceptible difference in the jamb mouldings between the upper and lower parts of each window. This said, the higher dressings appear to be of one build with the surrounding stonework, which in turn supports the bases of the intended windows of the unbuilt second floor. Taken as a whole, the evidence suggests that the entire build of the lower windows is unlikely to be any later than about 1330 — the date which marks the end of the main construction period.

As left at that time, the first-floor accommodation towards the courtyard appears to have comprised a single hall, approximately seventy feet by twenty-five feet (21.3m by 7.6m). The position of the two fireplaces, however, suggests that — as at Harlech — a dividing cross-wall was intended, probably on the line of the eastern side of the gate-passage below. Today, upper levels within the gatehouse can be reached and observed at various points. In particular, the newel stair in the south-west turret gives access all the way to the topmost level, and this same point may be reached via the wall-walk along the western curtain.

From this upper vantage point you will have a good view of the moulded corbels or brackets running down both sides of the hall. They presumably supported timber wall-posts used in the framing of the roof. Higher in the north and south walls, near the centre, you will also see a pair of 'springers' for a stone arch which would have supported the intended second floor. In the south wall, notice the bases of the embrasures and window seats of the five intended second-floor windows. And in the end wall(s), it is possible to see faint indications of the outline of the hall's low-pitched roof. There are, incidently, similar indications of the slope of the pent roof which covered as much as was built of the rooms in the two northern towers and over the gate-passage.

Back at ground level, looking up into the corners between the gatehouse and the adjacent curtain walls, you will see traces

A cutaway reconstruction of the north gatehouse to show the extent of the building as it may have been left in the 1330s. The upper parts (shown in outline) were never completed and the roofing arrangements were of necessity a makeshift compromise (Illustration by Chris Jones-Jenkins, 1999).

of the supports for wooden platforms. If these platforms were removed, the gate and the wall-walks could be isolated one from the other. On the west side, a modern access 'bridge' takes the place of the medieval platform. In this same corner, looking at the south-west stair turret, notice the door which communicated at first-floor level with the now-vanished range of buildings on the west side of the courtyard. As above, the access may have been by way of a removable timber platform.

Moving out from the inner ward to the north side of the gatehouse, you will see the large trefoil-headed windows which lit the three rooms on the upper floor. Below are the plainer lights of the lower chambers. There was a fireplace in each of the six rooms. In the case of the two examples over the gate-passage, this is an indication that they were not designed — as were the corresponding rooms at Harlech — to serve as chapels.

This general view across the inner ward shows the low foundations representing the back walls and turrets of the south gatehouse. Though planned on a similar scale to the north gatehouse, it appears the masonry never rose much above the level which survives today.

The overall concept behind the north gatehouse at Beaumaris was very similar to that employed at Harlech Castle some twelve years earlier.

THE SOUTH GATEHOUSE

It is clear that in all essentials the south gatehouse was planned to be the close counterpart of that to the north. In the symmetrical layout of the castle they are set axially opposite one another. But even though the part of the south gatehouse projecting into the courtyard may once have stood slightly higher than now (p. 15), it is certain that the building as a whole never achieved anything even approaching the degree of completeness of its far from finished northern replica. Whereas the great outward flanking towers of the north gatehouse were, as we have seen, carried up at least in part to their full intended height, those of the south gatehouse never rose beyond the level of the curtain walls to either side of them.

Thus, even towards the front, where the gatehouse is at its highest, we have to envisage the addition of a whole upper storey and battlements to the twin towers. The stair turrets towards the courtyard, now little more than shapeless stumps of masonry, would have risen to a height of something like seventy feet (21.3m). Small wonder that of the sum of £684 estimated to be needed for repairing and completing the castle in 1343, no less than £320 (£200 of it masons' work) was said to be required for the south gatehouse (p. 12).

THE WALL-PASSAGES

All of the inner ward curtain walls are pierced at the first-floor level by long passages, similar to those which are such a marked characteristic of Caernarfon Castle. Here at Beaumaris their purpose was to provide internal communication between the various rooms in the flanking towers of the inner ward, and also to give access to the latrines contrived beside them within the thickness of the walls (pp. 35–6). The passages are roofed with flat shouldered vaults composed of roughly shaped flag stones carried on running brackets corbelled out from the tops of the side walls. It is possibly these flagstones which are referred to in the 1296 Pipe Roll account as *petras velosas* ('sail stones'). Robert of Preston and his fellow boatmen brought some 19,706 tons of them by sea from the quarry to the castle in the summer of that year at a cost of 2*d.* a ton, a total of £164 4*s.* 4*d.*

The wall-passages in the inner ward curtain walls are roofed with flat-shouldered vaults composed of roughly shaped flag stones. This is a view along the passages on the west side of the inner ward.

Close beside the south-east tower is a small guardroom or sleeping chamber. Its roof is gathered over from no fewer than six courses of corbelling.

These passages can be reached today by the circular staircases leading up from the south-west and south-east corners of the inner ward. There are corresponding stairs in the two northern corners, and in the middle of the western side, but being partly ruined these latter are now inaccessible. Nor is the circuit of the passages any longer continuous, owing to the floors being destroyed in both the great north and south gatehouses.

To reach the eastern passage, you should follow the steps which lead up from the south-east corner of the courtyard. Inside, the left-hand door from the bottom landing leads to the newel staircase. At the next landing you should turn right again to gain access to the main east passage. This can be followed through to the east tower of the north gatehouse. First, however, close beside the south-east tower, notice the small guardroom or sleeping chamber in the thickness of the wall. The vaulted roof of this chamber is gathered over from no fewer than six courses of corbelling.

As you progress along the passage, you will find a succession of doorways leading off from the right, the first two giving access to latrines. Next there is a door to one of the chapel's side watching chambers. Then — down a short flight of steps — is the entrance to the chapel proper. The doorway to the second watching chamber is found beyond, and next to this is a spiral stair which led up to the wall-walk. From here, the narrowing of the passage on the left is where it passes behind the fireplaces of the adjacent great hall and chamber. Further on, near the north-east tower, there is another small guardroom with a corbelled vault. Finally, on the left, you will see the doors into another pair of latrines which

served both the tower and the eastern side of the north gatehouse.

Should you wish to follow the sequence in the western curtain wall, access to the passage is gained by way of the steps in the south-west corner of the courtyard. There are similar openings to latrines and wall chambers along the whole half circuit, from gatehouse to gatehouse.

THE CHAPEL

Meanwhile, as we have observed, the handsome little chapel royal occupies the first floor of that tower sited half-way along the eastern curtain wall. Even devoid of its medieval colour and fittings, it undoubtedly remains one of the highlights to be found at Beaumaris. To understand the original arrangements, it is best to begin by standing immediately outside the chapel proper.

Here, you are positioned in what was a small vestibule or lobby opening from the arched doorway towards the courtyard. Of course, the doorway itself was housed within the now lost range of buildings which ran just outside (pp. 26–7). In turn, further lobbies to the left and right of the vestibule led to watching chambers on each side of the chapel. These lobbies also communicated with the northern and southern halves of the wall-passage. The chapel was entered directly from the vestibule through the trefoil-headed twin doorways. At the appropriate times, the entire complex could be closed off from the remainder of the castle.

Within, the chapel has a polygonal east end and is covered with a ribbed-stone vault springing from semi-octagonal

The attractive little chapel royal at Beaumaris is situated on the first floor of the inner ward tower at the centre of the eastern curtain wall. Even devoid of its medieval colour and fittings, the chapel remains one of the highlights of the castle.

wall shafts. Above the remains of a stone bench, panels of triple blind arcading decorate the lower part of the walls, while the upper part contains five deeply set lancet windows. The openings in the north and south walls look out from the lateral watching chambers, and from the northern of which a squint has been cut to command a view of the altar. There are indications that an upper gallery existed at some time on the west side. And there is an air shaft sloping steeply upward in the west wall to the wall-walk above.

Outside the Chapel Tower, there is a small corbelled projection which may have housed a bell (p. 39). The chapel is built over a barrel-vaulted basement, while its own vault would have carried the floor of the tower's unfinished top storey, of which only a few feet of the walls were ever built. In 1343, the cost of completing it was estimated at £128, but work was evidently never resumed.

The chapel at Beaumaris was originally designed for the private use of the king and his family. In this manuscript illustration a royal lady holds back her curtain of privacy as a priest raises the Host during Mass (British Library, Yates Thompson Ms. 13, f. 7).

This cutaway reconstruction of the chapel at Beaumaris shows the ingenious arrangements in the overall design. When required, access from the wall-passages could be closed off. The king himself might enter the vestibule from the royal apartments situated at first-floor level in the foreground of this view. From the vestibule, he could climb the steps to the left to attend Mass in the small watching chamber (Illustration by Chris Jones-Jenkins, 1991).

THE FLANKING TOWERS

In all, in addition to the two gatehouses, six round or half-round towers flank the curtains of the inner ward. From the point at which you entered the castle, the south-east tower, Chapel Tower, and north-east towers lie to the right; the south-west tower, Middle Tower, and north-west towers are to the left. The Chapel Tower having already been described above, attention is here drawn to the principal features of the remaining towers.

Apart from the Chapel Tower, with its stone floor and vault, all the others towers are without roofs and floors of any kind. All were designed to be three storeys high, but the top storey was only partly built in the case of the three eastern towers, and to an even lesser extent in the case of those on the west. Internally, above a circular ground stage, the four corner towers are all octagonal. The Chapel Tower and Middle Tower have semi-octagonal interiors at all levels.

In the corner towers, the only light and air admitted to the circular basements was by way of a single vent shaft sloping steeply up through the thickness of the walls to a narrow slit. In short, they can only have been intended as prisons. Stone diaphragm arches (complete in the south-east tower and Middle Tower, with partial evidence in the south-west and north-east towers) may indicate an exceptionally strong and heavy floor above each basement. There is also a complete diaphragm arch over the main room in the north-east tower. The principal chamber in each tower was situated on the first or middle floor. It was lit by a two-light mullioned window — similar to the top-floor windows

The complete remains of the stone diaphragm arch in the south-east tower may indicate that an exceptionally strong and heavy floor was built above its basement. The basement probably served for storage or as a prison, with the principal chamber on the first floor.

at Conwy Castle — and warmed from a fine hooded fireplace. In every case, subordinate rooms and latrines were at hand. These were reached throughout this level by way of the connecting passages. Sufficient of the second-floor rooms was built in the south-east tower and Chapel Tower to show that they would have closely resembled those below them.

The principal chamber in the north-east tower was again situated on the first floor and was equipped with a fine hooded fireplace. The diaphragm arch indicates the intention for a further good room at second-floor level.

WALL-WALKS AND LATRINES

The staircase at the south-west corner of the courtyard may be used to reach the top of the western curtain wall. In fact, although not all is now accessible, the level of the wall-walks is maintained with little variation around the perimeters of the unfinished corner towers and those of the south gatehouse. The paving with beach pebbles dates from the time of the Office of Works renovations in the 1920s and 1930s, prior to which the wall tops supported a rich growth of trees and other vegetation. The remains of the battlements are fragmentary, with only six out of an original thirty-six merlons still retaining their complete loops.

But enough is left to show that — as at the other north Wales castles of Edward I — these were set at alternating levels of declination so as to give command over differing fields of fire.

The most conspicuous feature of the entire Beaumaris wall-walks (seen well here on the west side) is the presence of the latrines which are placed in pairs: two pairs to each of the long sides, and one to each of the four short northern and southern sides, making sixteen latrines in all at this level. There were also sixteen more latrines accessible from the wall-passages below. Their ingenious construction repays examination. In each case, within a total wall thickness of just under sixteen feet (4.9m), there is a large rectangular pit extending from below ground level to the wall-walk. Above the pits, on each floor, there is a pair of latrine seats set back to back, separated one from the other by a continuous rectangular ventilating shaft rising from the centre of the pit to the outside air. The design is unique to Beaumaris, and is almost certainly related to the fact that the castle is placed at sea level within a water-filled moat, allowing the pits to be scoured through channels now long blocked beneath the outer ward. In much the same way, channels

Above Left: A cutaway reconstruction to show the arrangements of one set of latrines within the curtain walls of the inner ward. The latrine cubicles were equipped with doors and wooden seats, and each pair was separated by a continuous ventilation shaft rising to the outside air (Illustration by Chris Jones-Jenkins, 1985; revised 1999).

Left: The ingenious planning of the back-to-back latrine cubicles may be seen from the wall-walk on the west curtain of the inner ward.

under the outer ward at Rhuddlan run from the latrine pits to discharge into the surrounding dry moat.

The open position of the latrines on the Beaumaris wall-walk allows us to see the planning of the individual cubicles. These are approached down an angled flight of six or more steps, at the bottom of which privacy was afforded by a door neatly rebated against the wall. In many cases,

the stumps of the door's iron hinges, carefully run in lead, can still be seen. Beyond the door is the latrine proper, the groove for its wooden seat set in the walls of a little recess, with the air shaft behind separating it from its immediately adjoining neighbour.

The latrines and their flushing system were already a cause of concern at the time of John de Metfield's survey of 1306. Amongst other serious

shortcomings (*grevuse defautes*) at the castle, it was reported that the 'little houses' (*petites mesones*) in the body of the castle badly needed roofing. In other words, then as now they were open to the sky. Their drains (*gutteres*) required repairing and mending, and the said houses needed to be cleansed of refuse (*fer' netto de ordure*), the ducts (*les issues*) of the latrines being full of water and filth.

PURPOSE OF THE CASTLE'S RESIDENTIAL ACCOMMODATION

Many visitors will doubtless pause to wonder for whom so much accommodation was planned and considered necessary at Beaumaris Castle: the great hall and chamber indicated by the fireplaces on the eastern side of the courtyard; not one but two similar halls and chambers (though only one of them was ever built) in the north gatehouse; five self-contained suites in all. Had they been completed, the twin towers of the two gatehouses, the four corner towers, the Middle Tower and the top of the Chapel Tower would have added another nineteen good rooms, all warmed and well lit and each with its private latrine along the passage. What was it all for?

A short answer would be to say that something of this order must have been what was envisaged in 1295 as providing the minimum required to accommodate the king and queen and their households, if the king should marry again, and if the court should wish to make a stay in Anglesey. And perhaps we should not attempt to look further than this. But we may remind ourselves that

From the first, the accommodation at Beaumaris was designed to house a large royal household when the occasion demanded. In this thirteenth-century French manuscript illustration, a king and queen entertain their guests in a great hall with servants in attendance (British Library, Royal Ms. 14 E III, f. 89).

Edward of Caernarfon (1284–1327) was now entering his twelfth year, and a time might not lie far ahead when it would be additionally convenient to have fitting apartments appropriate to a prince and princess and their attendant households, as well as to a king and future queen. There was also the constable of the castle, whether resident with his family or represented by a deputy.

And where, if not in Beaumaris Castle, was the office of the sheriff of Anglesey? Conwy, a walled town from the first, had its 'King's Hall', its 'Prince's Hall', its justiciar's lodging, its tower 'assigned for the lodging of the chamberlain', all of them outside the castle but within the protection of the town walls. In 1295 Beaumaris would have no walls for a century and more to come. Thus, may it be unreasonable to suggest that some of the chambers — perhaps some of the suites — in the castle were planned with corresponding needs and claims in mind? As to lesser officials, the little fireplaced rooms in the corner turrets of the outer ward and over the Gate next the Sea must have been well suited for the comfort and convenience of the porters and the janitors.

THE OUTER WARD

INTERNAL FEATURES

It is in the nature of a concentrically planned castle such as Beaumaris that, when we stand in the narrow outer ward, we can see on the one hand the massive external face of the great walls and towers of the inner ward, and on the other the inside of the lower walls and towers of the outer. It is proposed to begin, therefore, by pointing out some of the features worth noting when perambulating the inner wall, before turning attention to the outer. You should start at the south-west tower and proceed northwards.

Notice first that in all three western towers the large two-light windows are almost all blocked with stone. Only the south-east tower window is now both unblocked and retains its mullion. Although it seems likely that the corresponding windows in the north-east tower and the four gate towers have been unblocked, they have also lost their central mullions. In this context, we may also note that in the whole circuit of the castle's outer walls and towers, a great many of the arrowslits at ground level — no fewer than seventy-nine out of a total of 164 — are wholly or partially blocked. Indeed, it is likely that at some time in the history of Beaumaris this blocking of the outer curtain wall loops was universal. Such a security measure must date either from the

Glyn Dŵr troubles of around 1403–05, or from the Civil War in the seventeenth century, but there is now no evidence to suggest which.

Turning again to the inner curtain, we may be struck by the notable regularity of the moulded stone corbel table which runs around the full circuit at wall-top level. Each section of the corbel table gives a decorative finish that in some measure compensates for the evident incompleteness of the towers. Moving around to the northern part of the outer ward, good examples of evidence for the constructional use of inclined scaffold paths can be seen in the sloping lines of putlog holes in the eastern tower of the gatehouse; also in the north-east tower, and in the curtains to either side of it.

On the east side, in the south angle between the Chapel Tower and the curtain wall, there is a small corbelled projection. It was perhaps intended, like a similar feature at Rhuddlan, to house a bell. Then, continuing around the circuit, in the south-east tower you will see the unblocked first-floor window with its surviving mullion. Further on, notice the well-preserved carving of one of two gargoyle head spouts on the south wall of the barbican. The barbican itself, through which we passed at the beginning of the tour, was built as a hindrance to any possibility of an enemy rushing the main south gatehouse. The construction was undertaken at a time when not only the gatehouse itself was unfinished,

Standing within the narrow confines of the outer ward, on the one hand is the massive external face of the walls and towers of the inner circuit of defence, and on the other the inside of the lower walls and towers of the outer ring. In this view along the western side of the castle, the main south-west tower is in the foreground.

but the south outer curtain and Gate next the Sea may also very likely still have stood short of their full intended height.

Although it is simple enough in its symmetrical eight-sided layout, the outer curtain wall with its numerous flanking towers and two twin-towered gateways is

On the inner face of the outer curtain, there is a moulded stone corbel table which runs for the full circuit at wall-top level. This section is on the east side, with the steps lowering the level at the back of tower 9.

THE BOROUGH OF BEAUMARIS AND ITS DEFENCES

The borough of Beaumaris, founded by Edward I in association with the castle, whose constable was *ex officio* its mayor, was granted its charter on 15 September 1296. It was intended from the first to supersede the ancient and closely adjacent Welsh town of Llanfaes, whose inhabitants were removed to a new site, Newborough. The 132¼ burgage tenements listed in a survey of 1305 make Beaumaris the largest of the north Wales boroughs founded in and after 1278. From the beginning wine, especially from Gascony, was purchased for the other castles at Beaumaris, which soon became the economic centre, as Caernarfon was the administrative centre, of the principality. The greater part of north Wales commerce was concentrated here and distributed by coastal shipping to the other boroughs to be sold at their fairs and markets. We read in 1323 of 160 gallons of Spanish honey bought for the Beaumaris garrison, and salt, corn, beans, hides, cloth, goat and calf skins are among the commodities traded. It was thus, a few centuries later, that Sir John Wynn (d. 1627) of Gwydir could write, '*they were called the lawiers of Caern'von, the marchants of Bewmares,*

and the gent of Conwy': if Conwy was the social and Caernarfon the administrative capital of north Wales in the later Middle Ages, the commercial capital was undoubtedly Beaumaris.

Though walled eventually, Beaumaris, unlike Conwy and Caernarfon, was not provided with its town wall contemporaneously with the building of its castle. Such provision does, however, appear to have been envisaged from the beginning. Beside the path and bridge in front of the castle dock, there can be seen the thirteen-foot (3.9m) wide footings for a wall which at its south end inclines away to the west in the direction known to have been followed by the town wall when it afterwards came to be built. The indications are that these footings were laid at the same time as the building of the lower part of the adjacent outer curtain of the castle, that is in 1295, and that when it was decided, at an unknown date, that the town wall could not be built in the foreseeable future, its intended point of junction with the castle's Gate next the Sea was faced up to form a low square turret projecting out from the right-hand gate tower (p. 44). We

know that the burgesses were petitioning the king, without practical result, for their wall to be built in or about 1315.

It was not until after the town had suffered heavily in the Glyn Dŵr troubles at the beginning of the fifteenth century that action to remedy the lack of a town wall was finally taken. The castle seems to have fallen to the Welsh in 1403 and was not recovered until 1405. We have a record that in 1407 the burgesses were granted £10 towards the cost of circling the town with a bank and ditch (*in auxilium faciendi fossam circa villam*). The building of the stone wall appears to have followed within seven years, for another record, of 1414, implies that thirty burgages have been requisitioned to make way for it (*causa nove edificacionis novi muri circa eandem villam*) so that the customary rent could no longer be obtained for them. The need for a wall to enclose and protect the town is shown by a record of 1408–09 explaining that there were 10½ burgages for which no rent could be collected, because they had been destroyed by fire not only by the Welsh rebels under Glyn Dŵr but also by the Scots (*eo quod combusta et*

none the less a complex and remarkable piece of construction. It is remarkable in particular for the completeness of its survival, in contrast to the fragmentary state of the corresponding works at Aberystwyth, Harlech and Rhuddlan. In Wales, at least, Beaumaris stands as the concentric castle *par excellence*.

As a further obstacle to attack, the outer curtain also had an offensive purpose. In fact, its arrowloops provided firing points in every direction at three levels from the turrets and two from the linking sections of wall. The crenellation, or the battlementing with the top level of loops, has almost entirely perished. But it is calculated that when complete this outer circuit of fortification was equipped with not far short of 300 firing positions. From any group of these, the defending garrison could harass attackers at whatever point they might concentrate their assault.

The survey of 1343 (pp. 14–15) reported thirty perches of the castle walls as being 'partly ruinous'. If the reference was to the outer curtain, it may be that the section strengthened by the addition of internal arches to the west of the Gate next the Sea was included, and that the arches are a remedial measure carried out at that time. It is noticeable that the length of wall eastwards from the Gate next the Sea to the south-east corner shows a slight inward lean, but these two lengths together are still a good deal short of thirty perches.

destructa fuerunt tam per rebellos Wallenses quam per Scoticos).

Only fragmentary portions of the wall remain today; its three gates have all vanished, as have its presumed flanking towers. It is clear that the wall was provided with battlements and latrines, and that there were passages in it. As early as 1414 ten burgages are recorded as being submerged by the sea, and in 1460 the wall itself is described as completely broken by the waves; but rebuilding is known to have been carried out between 1536 and 1540, and the Corporation carried out repairs during the late seventeenth and early eighteenth centuries. The West Gate was still standing as late as 1785.

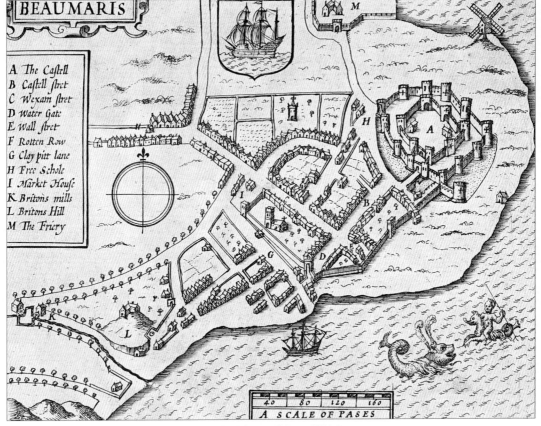

John Speed's 1610 plan of the castle and borough of Beaumaris (National Library of Wales).

A general view along the length of the western side of the outer curtain wall. Towers 15 and 16 in the foreground probably belong to the second phase of construction, after 1306.

EXTERIOR OF OUTER WARD

From the February 1296 report of progress on the castle (pp. 8–9), it would seem that only ten of the outer turrets were included in the initial construction works begun in the previous year. And, looking carefully from the exterior the castle, you will be able to detect the points at which this earliest construction was subsequently linked with later work, and heightened throughout to produce the outer curtain as we see it today. As a whole, the outer curtain can be viewed from across the moat on the north, the west and south-west sides, and from the recreation ground outside the castle on the east.

The ten towers mentioned in the record of 1296 commence with the tower numbered 1 on the plan at the end of the guide, and continue anticlockwise to the tower numbered 10 at the north-east corner. The first work appears to have reached a height of only about eight feet (2.4m) above the water level in the moat. For much of the intervening distance there is a well-marked horizontal break or change-line in the masonry. Everywhere below this line the arrowloops are distinctive in having dressed stone jambs, or sides, but no dressed stone lintel. Above it, the loops on all the towers, and throughout the section subsequently built to complete the circuit on the north and west (stretching from tower 10 back to tower 1), have dressed stone lintels as well as dressed jambs and bases. All this later work must belong to the period after 1306 and before 1330, but it cannot be dated more closely.

LLANFAES GATE

It appears that the proposed outer gatehouse on the north side of the castle, namely the Llanfaes Gate, also belongs to those works undertaken by Master Nicholas of Derneford after 1306. In 1330 — when construction at Beaumaris seems finally to have ceased — it was to remain unfinished, probably in a condition not so very dissimilar from that observed today. The best position to see the various details is from the bank on the opposite side of the moat, though visitors should be aware that the path becomes a little narrow towards the end.

It was originally designed as a smaller version of the main north and south gatehouses, with a central gate-passage, marked by inner and outer arches, flanked by a projecting tower to each side. There is evidence for a portcullis, and the passage would have been further defended from arrowloops in the side walls. The walls of the proposed towers project irregularly and have been roughly faced off at the outer ends. At some point, arches were struck across them at a high level to carry a somewhat improvised wall-walk.

Two examples of the arrowloops in the outer curtain wall. That to the left is without a dressed stone lintel and is situated below the horizontal constructional break in the masonry. The arrowloop to the right has a dressed stone lintel, jambs and base, and is situated above the same horizontal break.

The proposed outer gatehouse on the north side of the castle is known as the Llanfaes Gate. It was probably one of the works begun after 1306 and was to be a smaller version of the main north and south gatehouses. When construction of Beaumaris finally ended in the 1330s, the Llanfaes gate remained incomplete, very much as it appears today.

CASTLE DOCK AND GUNNERS WALK

From the 1296 report (pp.8–9), it is clear that the dock was planned from the beginning of the building works. It was intended to make the castle directly accessible to seagoing shipping, the door in its end wall enabling a boat to unload straight into the outer ward.

The flanking wall to the east, known from the mid-nineteenth century as 'Gunners Walk', was built to revet this side of the dock. The wall-top afforded a shooting deck with arrowloops and battlements on either side of the twelve foot (3.7m) thickness. A raised and 'machicolated' platform at its southern end may well have been the position of a trebuchet, or stone-throwing catapult.

The tower which projects from Gunners Walk into the dock contains the remains of a watermill, together with the sluice controlling the flow of tidal water to and from the moat.

Known from the mid-nineteenth century as the 'Gunners Walk', the flanking wall to the east of the castle dock afforded a shooting deck with battlements on either side. The 'machicolated' platform at its southern end may have been the position of a trebuchet, or stone-throwing engine of war.

FURTHER READING

A. D. Carr, *Medieval Anglesey* (Llangefni 1982).

H. Rees Davies, *The Conway and the Menai Ferries* (Cardiff 1942).

R. R. Davies, *Conquest, Coexistence and Change: Wales 1063–1415* (Oxford 1987); reprinted in paperback as, *The Age of Conquest: Wales 1063–1415* (Oxford 1991).

R. R. Davies, *The Revolt of Owain Glyn Dŵr* (Oxford 1995).

J. Goronwy Edwards, 'Edward I's Castle-Building in Wales', *Proceedings of the British Academy*, **32** (1946), 15–81.

Colin M. Evans, *The Medieval Borough of Beaumaris and the Commote of Dindaethwy, 1200–1600* (Unpublished MA Thesis, University of Wales Bangor 1949).

The Royal Commission on Ancient & Historical Monuments in Wales & Monmouthshire, *An Inventory of the Ancient Monuments in Anglesey* (London 1937), cxlviii–cxlix, 1–14.

Edward Arthur Lewis, *The Mediæval Boroughs of Snowdonia* (London 1912).

J. E. Morris, *The Welsh Wars of Edward I* (Oxford 1901); reprinted (Stroud 1997).

E. Neaverson, *Mediaeval Castles in North Wales: A Study of Sites, Water Supply and Building Stones* (Liverpool and London 1947), 50-51.

Michael Prestwich, *Edward I* (London 1988).

A. J. Taylor, *The King's Works in Wales, 1277–1330* (London 1974); reprinted as, Arnold Taylor, *The Welsh Castles of Edward I* (London 1986).

A. J. Taylor, 'Castle-Building in Thirteenth-Century Wales and Savoy', *Proceedings of the British Academy*, **63** (1977), 265–92.

Arnold Taylor, *Four Great Castles* (Newtown 1983).

Arnold Taylor, 'The Beaumaris Castle Building Account of 1295–1298', in John R. Kenyon and Richard Avent (editors), *Castles in Wales and the Marches* (Cardiff 1987), 125–42.